OCEAN ANIMALS
STICKER ACTIVITY BOOK

Pull out the sticker sheets an̶
them b̶
use ̶   anywhere you want

NATIONAL GEOGRAPHIC
Washington, D.C.

Consultant: Jack Sewell
Editorial, Design, and Production by

make believe ideas

Picture credits: All images Shutterstock unless noted as follows:
Corbis: 20 tr; ml, 29 tr, **Stephen Frink:** 30 m (Atlantic spotted dolphins),
Make Believe Ideas: 1 mr, 2 br, 3 tl, 6 ml; br (sea star x 3),
15 mr, 18 tr; bl (yellow fish x 2); mr (clown fish), 19 ml (large stingray);
bl (side-on stingray x 4), 22 br (crab), 24 br; bl, 25 ml (yellow fish),
NGS: 19 br (stingray x 4), 21 br, 24 m.

Sticker pages: All images Shutterstock unless noted as follows:
Corbis: 20, 21 hatchet fish; anglerfish, **Make Believe Ideas:** 2, 3 jellyfish; yellow fish,
4, 5 jellyfish, 6, 7 sea star, 8, 9 small turtle x 2, Extra stickers (sheet 4) crab,
18, 19 blue-spotted stingray; side-on stingray x 4, 28, 29 silver fish; crab; squid,
Extra stickers (sheet 5) orange fish x 12, Extra stickers (sheet 6) blue-spotted stingray,
NGS: 18, 19 large stingray x 5; side-on stingray x 6, 24, 25 hammerhead shark.

Printed in China. 18/MBI/3

The coral reef is full of colors!

Coral reefs are made up of tiny sea animals called polyps.

polyps

Sticker more fish.

Sponges are really animals!

A clownfish will live safely inside an anemone's tentacles. The anemone eats scraps from the clownfish's meals.

Sticker clownfish around the anemone.

Tropical fish are brightly colored.

butterflyfish

coral hind

queen angelfish

parrot fish

Seahorses are weak swimmers, so they often wrap their tails around sea grass to keep steady.

Copy the seahorse. Use the grid to help you.

white-spotted pufferfish

Pufferfish and porcupinefish "puff" up their bodies with water to look bigger. This scares away fish that might eat them.

porcupinefish

porcupinefish

Use stickers to finish the patterns.

Sea stars and urchins live on the **sea floor.**

bat star

If a sea star loses an arm, it can grow a new one!

cushion sea star

 Find your way through the sea-star maze.

Start

Finish

Most urchins have sharp spikes all over their bodies. Their name means "sea hedgehog."

Sticker spikes on the urchin.

fire urchin

collector urchin

slate pencil urchin

Draw lines to join the matching pairs of sea urchins.

Sea turtles have shells!

Turtles lay their eggs in holes in the sand. When the baby turtles hatch, they crawl back to the sea.

hawksbill turtle

baby green sea turtle

loggerhead turtle

Follow the lines to find out which baby turtle reaches the sea first.

Use the key to color the turtle.

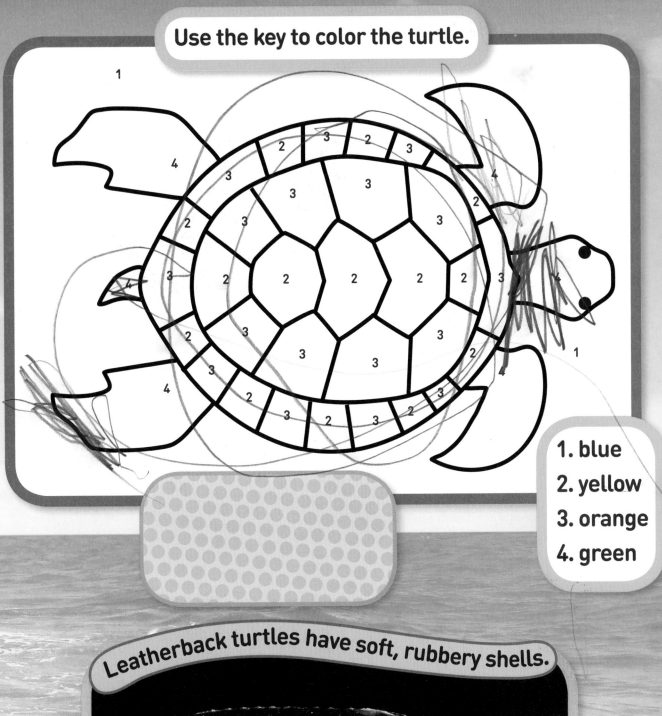

1. blue
2. yellow
3. orange
4. green

Leatherback turtles have soft, rubbery shells.

Sea slugs and clams have soft bodies.

Color the nudibranch.

Nudibranchs are a type of sea slug. They use the tentacles on their bodies to touch, taste, and smell.

Find the missing stickers, then draw lines to match the pairs of nudibranchs.

The giant clam can grow to be almost as big as a six-year-old kid!

giant clam

Add them up!

2 + 3 =

3 + 4 =

Crabs and lobsters have strong claws!

Sally Lightfoot crab

Crabs usually walk sideways because of the shape of their legs.

porcelain crab

land crab

Sticker the claws on the crab.

Lobsters live in burrows or in rocks to keep hidden.

Help the lobster through the maze to find its burrow.

Start

Finish

Jellyfish have long tentacles!

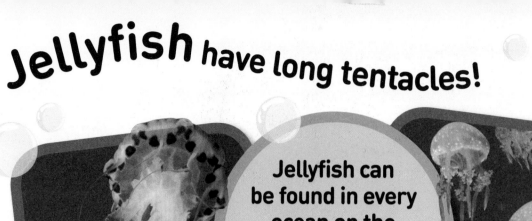

Jellyfish can be found in every ocean on the planet—from shallow reefs to the deep sea!

purple-striped jellyfish

Australian spotted jellyfish

crown jellyfish

flower hat jellyfish

Draw more tentacles on the jellyfish.

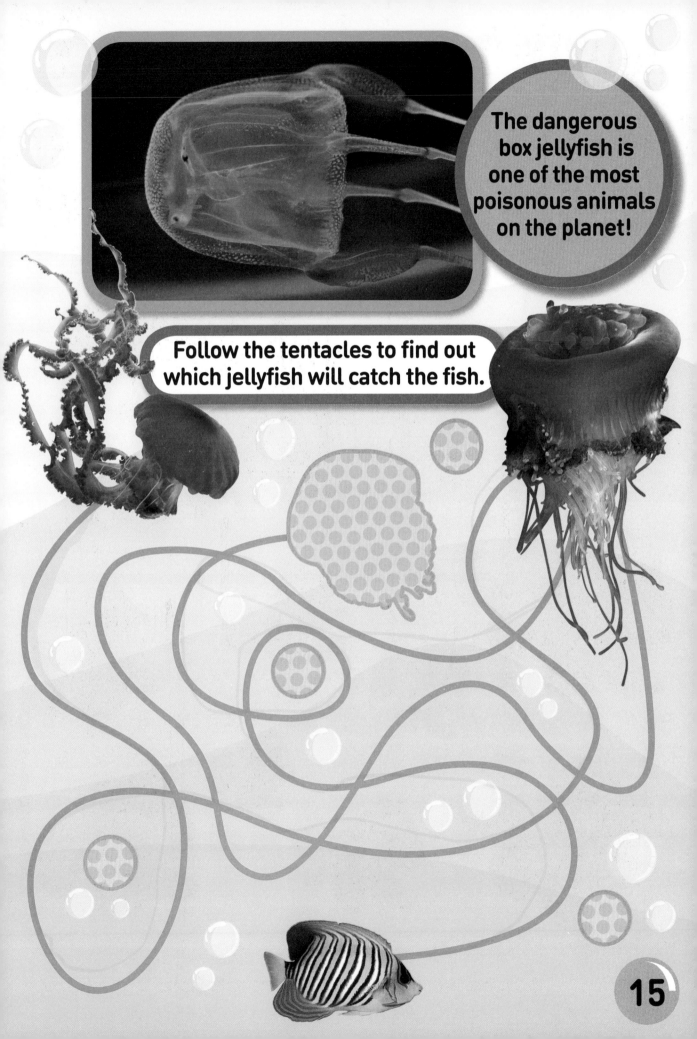

The dangerous box jellyfish is one of the most poisonous animals on the planet!

Follow the tentacles to find out which jellyfish will catch the fish.

Octopuses and squid have **many** arms!

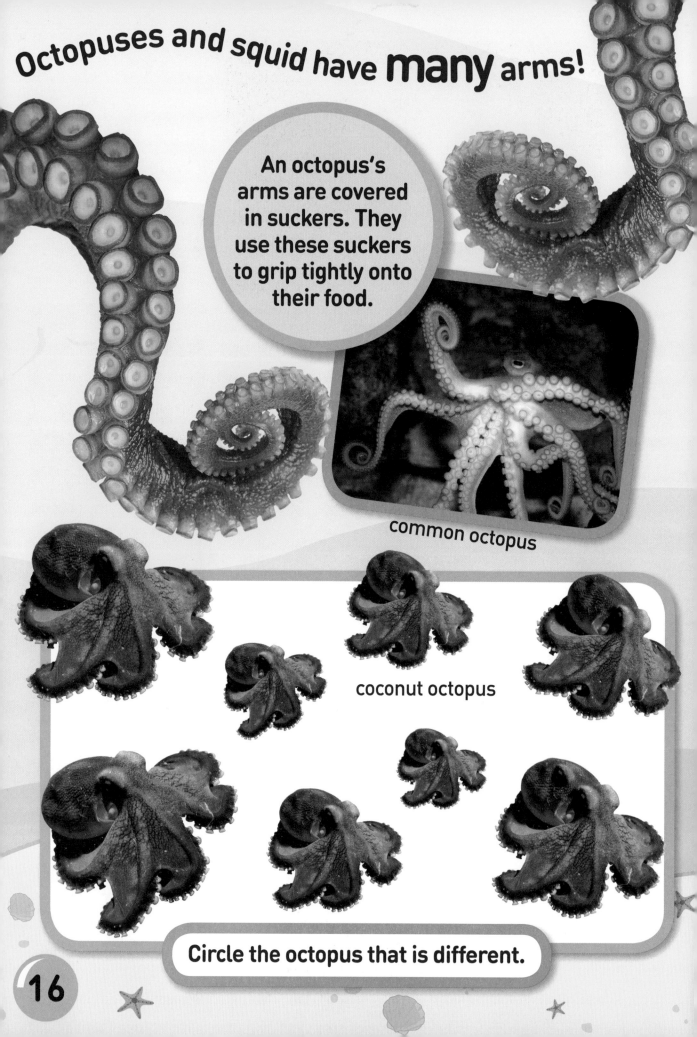

An octopus's arms are covered in suckers. They use these suckers to grip tightly onto their food.

common octopus

coconut octopus

Circle the octopus that is different.

bobtail squid

Squid can change the color of their skin, making them appear almost invisible!

reef squid

Can you circle five squid hiding in the picture?

Rays have flat bodies and large fins.

Oceanic manta rays swim with enough power to jump out of the ocean and land with big belly flops!

manta ray

manta ray

Color the manta ray.

yellow stingray

Stingrays use the stingers on their tails for self-defense.

bluespotted ray

stingray

Add them up!

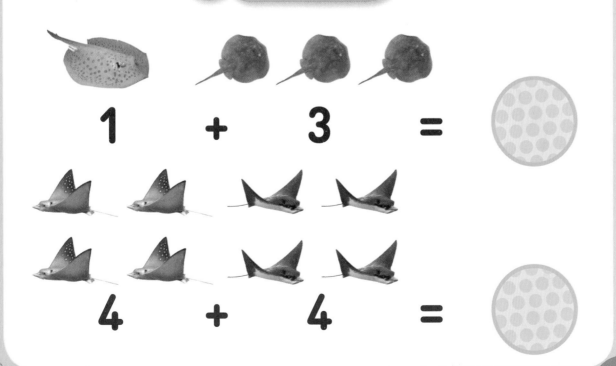

1 + 3 =

4 + 4 =

The deep sea is home to **cool** creatures!

Lanternfish have organs that make light. These lights help the fish recognize each other—even in the dark, deep sea!

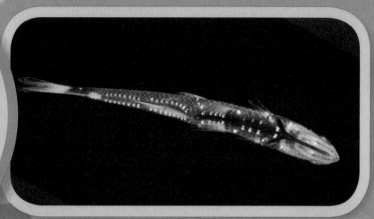

lanternfish

There are lots of other fish that make light!

flashlight fish

deep-sea hatchet fish

anglerfish

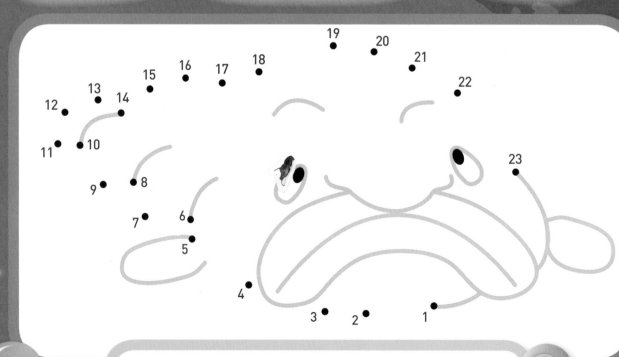

Connect the dots to finish the blobfish.

Stickers for pages 2 and 3

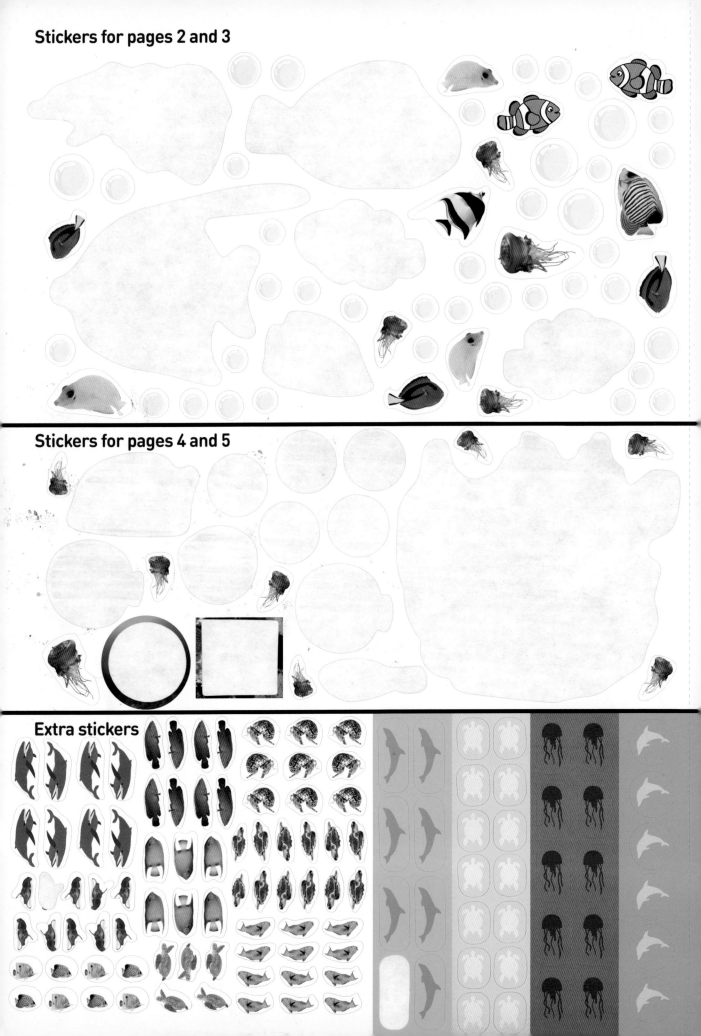

Stickers for pages 4 and 5

Extra stickers

Stickers for pages 6 and 7

Stickers for pages 8 and 9

Extra stickers

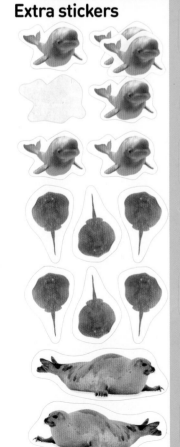

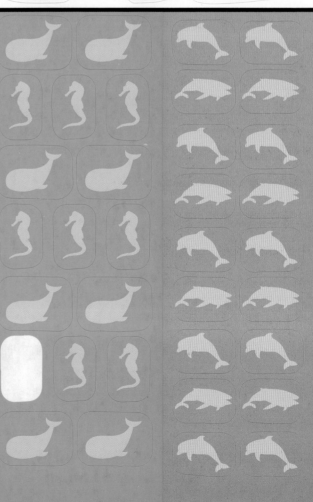

Stickers for pages 10 and 11

Stickers for pages 12 and 13

Extra stickers

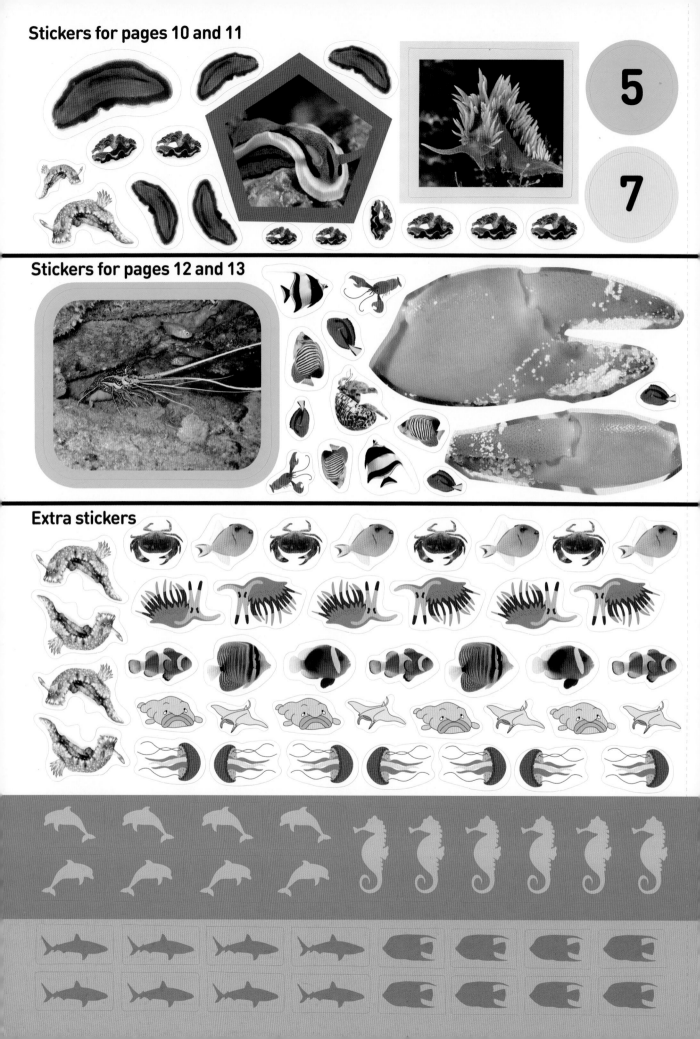

Stickers for pages 14 and 15

Stickers for pages 16 and 17

Stickers for pages 18 and 19

4 8

Extra stickers

Stickers for pages 20 and 21

Stickers for pages 22 and 23

Stickers for pages 24 and 25

Extra stickers

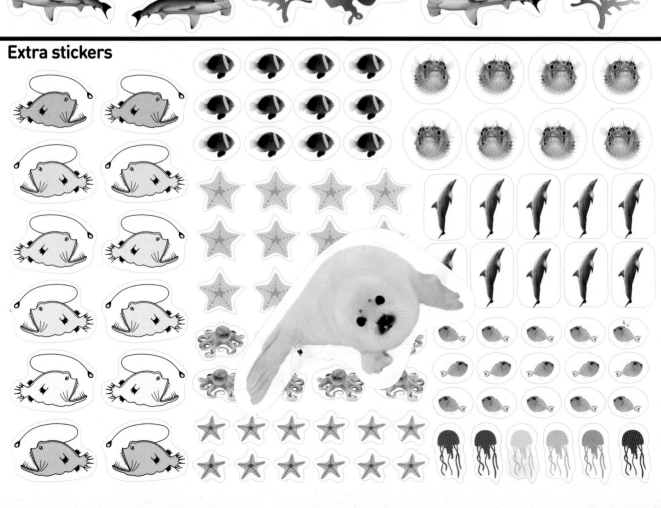

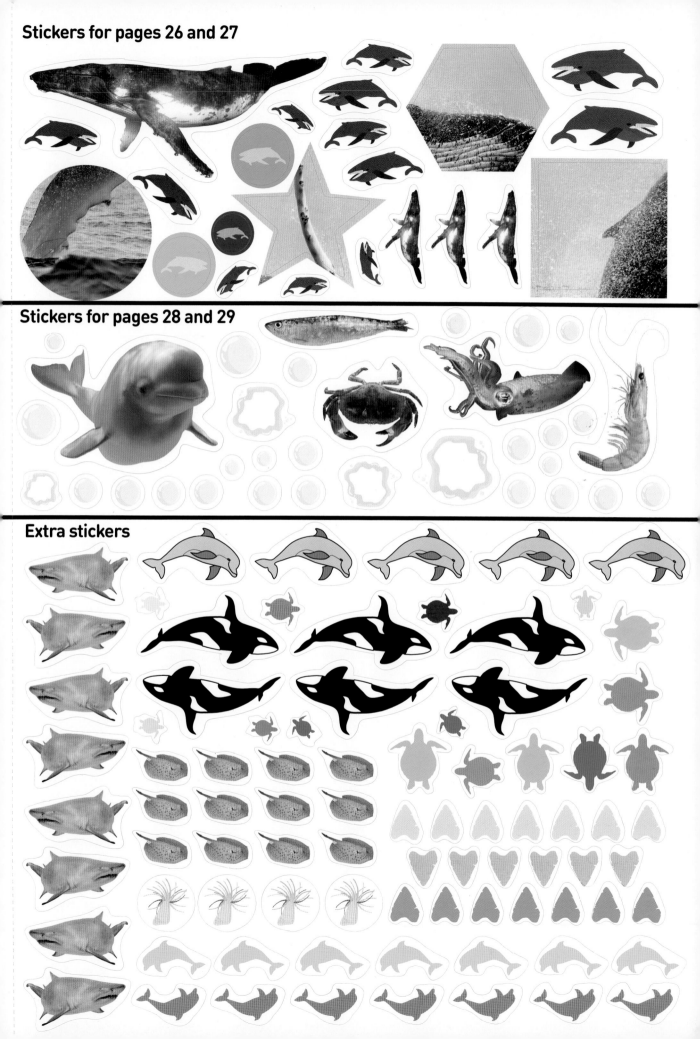

Stickers for pages 26 and 27

Stickers for pages 28 and 29

Extra stickers

Stickers for pages 30 and 31

Stickers for pages 32 and 33

Stickers for pages 34 and 35

Stickers for pages 36 and 37

Stickers for pages 38 and 39

Stickers for page 40

Extra stickers

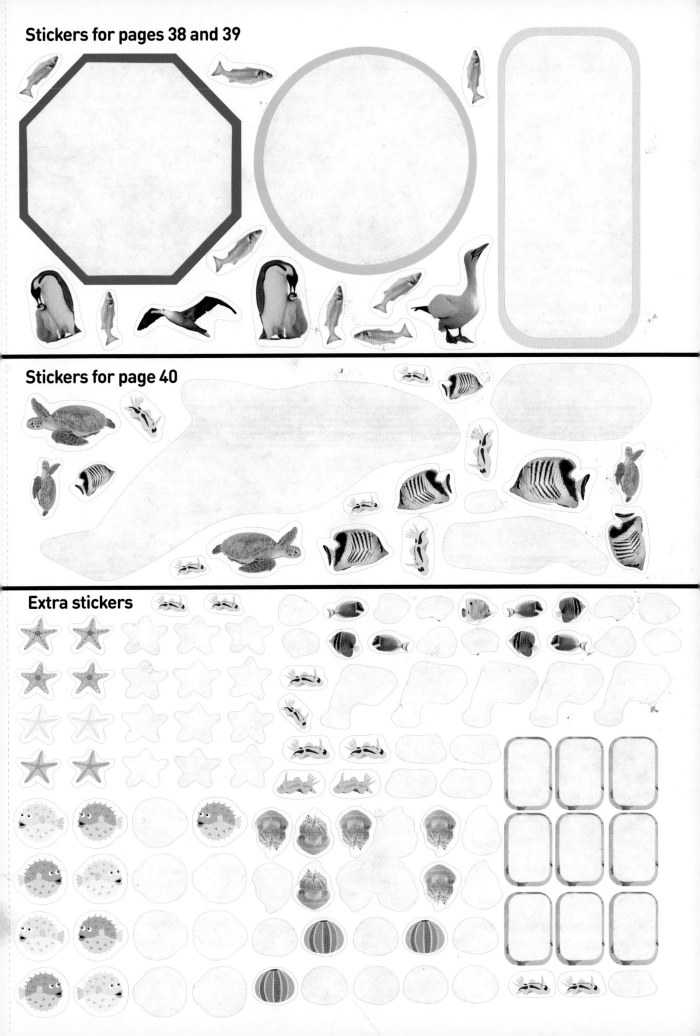

Color the anglerfish.

A female anglerfish's mouth is so big that she can eat fish up to twice her size!

Sharks have lots of teeth!

A shark's teeth are arranged in rows. When a tooth falls out, another tooth moves forward to replace it!

lemon shark

Sticker more teeth!

sand tiger shark

Find six differences between the pictures.

Great white sharks don't chew their food—they swallow it whole or in large chunks!

Help the shark through the maze to catch the fish.

Start

great white shark

Finish

Sharks can be unusual shapes!

Hammerhead sharks get their name from the shape of their amazing heads!

Follow the lines to find out what the hammerhead shark wants for dinner.

The tasseled wobbegong shark has a beard made of whiskers that look like seaweed.

Find all five words to finish the word search.

shark • tooth • saw • head • sea

s	e	a	u	e	p
t	h	b	k	i	f
o	d	a	x	q	h
o	t	s	r	m	e
t	g	a	z	k	a
h	z	w	n	y	d

Baleen whales are gentle giants.

Baleen whales have bristles, called baleen, instead of teeth. Humpback whales, blue whales, and minke whales all have baleen.

Circle the whale that is different.

Despite weighing up to 33 tons, enormous humpback whales can jump clear out of the water. This is called breaching.

humpback whale

Find the missing stickers to finish the picture.

Toothed whales hunt for food!

sperm whale

Toothed whales have teeth and hunt for food that they can chew! Sperm whales, pilot whales, and belugas are all toothed whales.

beluga

Sticker food for the whale.

Belugas often play together. They especially like to blow bubble rings!

Draw more bubble rings for the belugas to play with.

Dolphins and porpoises are a type of whale!

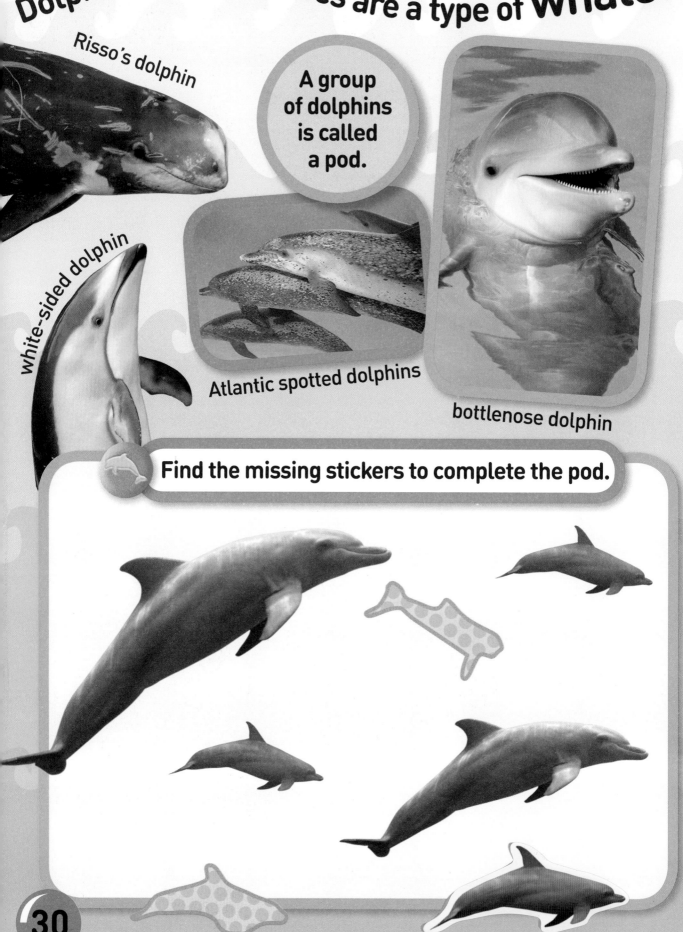

Risso's dolphin

A group of dolphins is called a pod.

white-sided dolphin

Atlantic spotted dolphins

bottlenose dolphin

Find the missing stickers to complete the pod.

Connect the dots to finish the orca.

orca

Orcas are the largest dolphins in the world!

Dugongs and manatees eat sea grass!

Dugongs and manatees use their sensitive snouts to search for sea grass on the sea floor.

dugong

manatee

Find the missing stickers to finish the picture.

manatees

Draw sea grass for the manatee to eat.

Manatees spend about half of every day asleep.

Some lizards and snakes live in the sea!

The marine iguana is the only lizard today that can dive into the sea to find food.

marine iguana

Circle the sea snake that is different.

banded sea snake

Male saltwater crocodiles can grow to be 20.7 ft (6.3 m) long, making them the largest living reptiles!

saltwater crocodile

Color the crocodile.

Seals and Otters have fur!

Baby harp seals, or pups, have soft, white fur. A mother can tell which pup is hers partly by the way it smells.

Help the harp seal through the maze to find her pup.

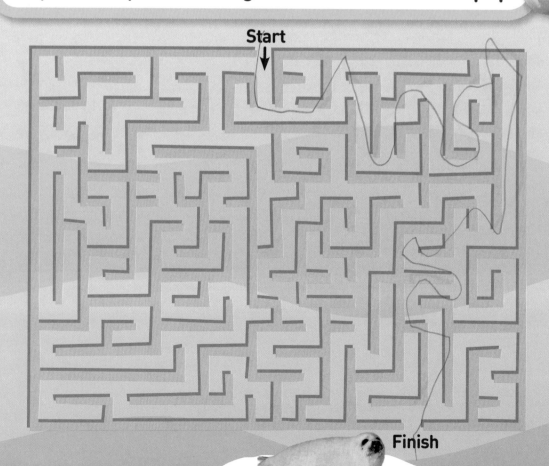

Start

Finish

Sea otters often hold paws when sleeping so they don't drift away from each other.

Count how many of each thing you can find in the picture.

Find the missing stickers.

sunglasses ....

baseball cap ....

37

Sea **birds** live by the ocean.

Find the missing stickers.

Penguins cannot fly—they use their wings as flippers for fast swimming!

humboldt penguin

fairy penguin

chinstrap penguins

rockhopper penguin

gentoo penguin

emperor penguin

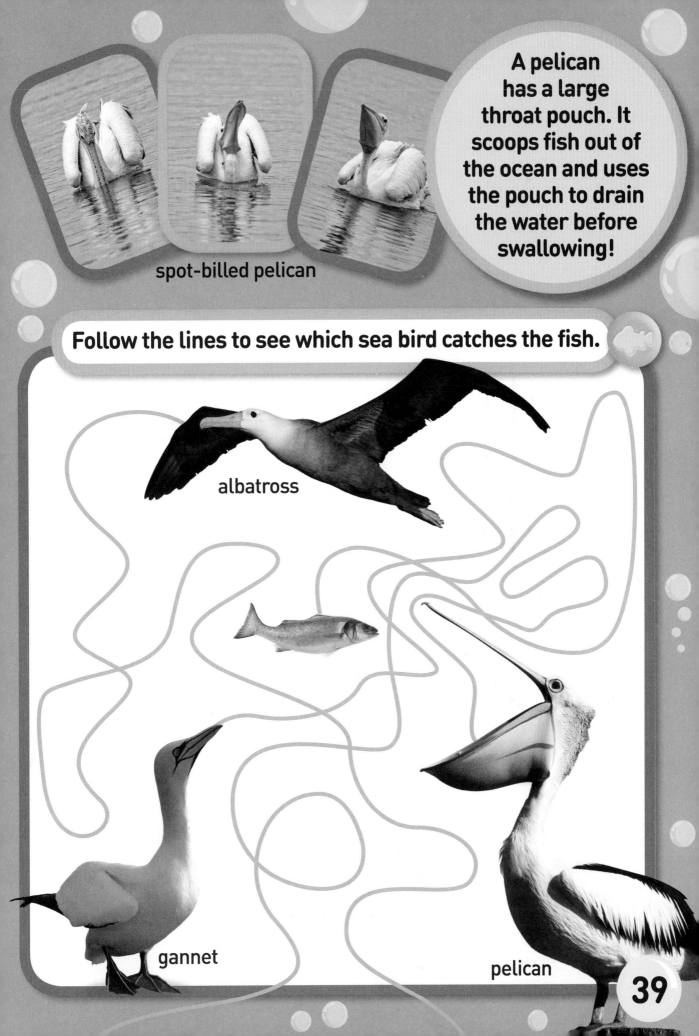

spot-billed pelican

A pelican has a large throat pouch. It scoops fish out of the ocean and uses the pouch to drain the water before swallowing!

Follow the lines to see which sea bird catches the fish.

albatross

gannet

pelican

Draw your **favorite** ocean animal here!

Find the missing stickers.